Be the
Light

ADAM A. BLOOM

Archway Publishing books may be ordered through booksellers or by contacting:

Archway Publishing
1663 Liberty Drive
Bloomington, IN 47403
www.archwaypublishing.com
1 (888) 242-5904

ISBN: 978-1-4808-7306-3 (sc)
ISBN: 978-1-4808-7307-0 (e)

Library of Congress Control Number: 2018914788

Print information available on the last page.

Archway Publishing rev. date: 12/19/2018

This book is dedicated to all those with love and hope for all of humanity and the life among us.

CONTENTS

INTRODUCTION

Being a man who suffers from both bipolar disorder and Crohn's disease, I needed a way to channel all the positive and negative energies and keep hope alive. I found poetry was the purest form of art to accomplish that. The combination of the two—one physical, the other psychological with emotional suffering—created the perfect storm whenever my Crohn's flared. My mind became a battleground of multiple health issues chronically testing my resolve and my hope, creating this feeling of constant turmoil and fear that it wouldn't end. I see a similar chaos in the world pulling my attention outward, which inspires me to raise my voice and speak out against forces old and new that keep us from a better reality.

You must push on. Life's adversity varies from soul to soul, but we have all felt some level of pain, and we have all felt joy and love to some extent. I tend to believe pain is currently overpowering love, making takers out of most of us, and there are people responsible, both directly and indirectly, for this imbalance.

Part of the problem is with varying levels of suffering and wealth, there are different recovery times and qualities. So we differ in another aspect: empathy. It seems all people learn some level of empathy once they have suffered, and perhaps many would need to suffer for the ego to reflect upon the body's vulnerabilities to develop empathy. But I am not suggesting people need to suffer more. We've had enough of our own abuses upon each other and would only benefit to move forward with respect and patience. It starts with holding ourselves accountable for what we've done, letting each other be human, and letting go of the past. This is done simultaneously with big change at the top, but we all need to work together in the healing process.

On the other hand, we need to be grateful for all we have, including a touch of time to change, normal weather when it happens, and of course, love. And with our technology, comes a freedom to reflect upon our true natures as sentient beings, and discover and develop more ideas about where and how we choose to move forward. It is not the time to be complacent. I hope to inspire and be another voice to encourage us to be better to ourselves, our world, and each other.

I

Chasing Truth

I have seen enough of human tendencies and institutions to know there are many fundamental issues with our civilization that will stifle our progress or end us altogether. Coupled with technology and its far-reaching capabilities, awareness and enlightenment are spreading faster and faster with an advantage that is sometimes a disadvantage—the division of knowledge, division orchestrated by powerful but extremely shortsighted people who distract us while they rape and swipe our resources.

This division is their victory as they have enough people believing in them to keep their versions of reality afloat, while the rest of us are distracted by myriad issues ranging from the mildly inappropriate to the possibly criminal. One thing is certain: they need us quarrelling and losing love as it gives them more power over us—more power to rape our environment, to pillage our resources, and to capture and uproot our most evolved and tested knowledge.

Sayings like, "It's only business," and, "It's nothing personal," negate natural empathy and give many without scruples license to trample. Now, you could say this is the modernization of survival of the fittest, but that is an excuse to continue the abuses; just more power and wealth to have more power and wealth. Empty pursuits until death, these are two things only gained at another's loss for the ultimate zero-sum game.

Power is an accumulation of the communal will of humans and has increased exponentially over the centuries, especially given world travel and globalization. We instantly communicate over the internet with people all over the world who are living similarly powerless lives. Beyond the power to choose certain basic freedoms is a loss of our say in the direction of where and how we, as a species, can or should all move forward. War is the barbarian's game, still necessary to defend because of different beliefs and cultures. But we need to realize that globally we are one. Wealth is not a vital part of happiness, but it may shield many discomforts and dangers that are otherwise unavoidable. Purpose and function in life are quite essential, so would a better society concentrate on those for each person, given automation should secure millions of jobs in the next decade or so?

Pleading with the Fallen Heart

Borne of rugged strife,
Of struggle and pain,
A life strained uneasy,
A changing world unchained.
But out of chaos
What seems of light,
A promise of heaven's sweet relief.
To falsely avenge your reality's tricks
Is the bringer of death.
More pain, no eternity,
Existence that doesn't.
A shadow, a memory maybe,
Gone without understanding.
Those in the path,
Rights waived,
Lives taken,
Sadness given.
Your pain is not forever.
But temporary or not,
The solution is not on your plate.
Believe not the voice of destruction.

Us All

What now resides within all quiet shores,
    A belief—us versus them—endures.
    Each man's view as though his path heaven sent,
    Rife with behaviors gone without repent.
    The other man always seen as stranger,
    Different outside, whole of love endangered.
    We often see false substance taken real.
    Hard, selfish ripeness driving hate's vast appeal.
Forthwith, humans frozen in their cores,
    Distances built, patience lost pours.
    Many wield power to keep wills gone spent,
    No longer slaves by fear's awesome intent,
    But still alive and lush of anger.
    Ready to fly, planes exit hangars,
    Dropping bombs to confirm the death they deal,
    Then justify innocent life they steal.
Resilience flows inside. A spirit soars,
    Though tempted by strong, hateful man's lures.
    A free soul freed that is no longer bent,
    Aware, flush within discovering truth sent.
    To embrace the coin's accord and danger,
    Not enough just to know this world changer.
    Accept in common to self, did deal,
    Birth proof that man's resolve of hate shan't anneal.

Be the Light

If you ever find
It's all up to you
To make a choice,
Then seek the truth.
The darkness pulls;
Will bring on fear.
What shows your grit
Is where you'll steer.
Don't quit. Don't fade.
Will through your fight.
Hate to hell be damned,
And be the light!

Take a second thought.
Your world is vast; ours too.
Get it together.

Hope is a hider
Even from the most valiant.
Free you anyway.

Leeches

Oh, loving capitalist,
You need and want too much
Then give and lend too little.
Does it have to be as such?
Building up to the moon,
Assigning cog and drone,
Leaving no room for dreaming.
Wouldn't dare throw 'em a bone.
We're pestered and pushed so much
By me, on the other end
Of a phone, driven by greed.
Have you tried the latest trend?
So I curse and deny it.
The obvious truth I see
Is I'm a sucking leech too,
Like every other man be.

At the Top

For all the full purses,
Tummies, and garages
That see the suffering
Neediness as mirages,
You insist it's just a game
When all is obtained
To take what someone else
Worked, dug in for and gained.
Your grubby hands don't stop,
And you'll still take mine
Because your stash won't do
Unless you become kind.
The truth will come to light
For even the blindest
Would eyes open huge,
May follow the kindest.
The wrath will come to thee
All in time, too damn late.
When nothing to be done,
We're all left the same fate.
So keep earning, hustling,
Corralling, and taking.
Without your sacrifice,
Reality is breaking.

Purging Waste

The path now cumbersome,
Cluttered exponential.
Just your needs attended.
No dreams essential.
Each day plenty different,
Trapped energies adrift.
Storage of waste gets old.
Force inner gears to shift,
Channel, and transform.
Time still passes by.
Look deep and gather.
Real truth never dies.
Let go the remainder.
Straining your aura,
Meditate openness
With fauna and flora.

Greed tips the balance.
Followers gladly follow.
Most left with hunger.

Willingness is key.
Not a strong-armed sacrifice.
Taxes no longer?

2118

To my beloved, sacred world,
One and only, single home.
Many will be desperate
When sun scorches full tone.
Most will suffer great loss.
Souls remain to wander
A barren rock uncared for,
Eternity left to ponder.
Heavy baggage from my time
When our supreme US,
Divided by evil lies,
Helped usher in this mess.
Though many species cared
With blind love from fear,
Even they know it's over
Unless we too hold life dear.
In my time, many claimed
The world's an ugly place
Just to sustain consumption.
'Cause it's truth we cannot face.
So make this planet your all,
Propping up all life left,
As sufferings most endured
Show our mutual theft.

Need

Those in need do need.
Most unable to rise
Deserve to live too,
Not just about a prize.
But no layabouts.
With sacrifices made,
There is a transfer
Of energy paid.
No free for free,
But the top secured.
We need sacrifice bunts,
Or riots be conjured.

Persevere

Driven fears awaken strong,
Promises well and good,
Arouse your hope brightly.
Take notice—you could.
To give in and be scared,
A show that's sure to end.
Finite, all is in truth,
Whatever you intend.
Count on all to pass
Sure as the sun comes up.
So watch your fall, and
Don't drink from fear's cup.
Go forth brave and aware.
Embrace all, good and bad.
Let the negative go
And all that makes you sad.
Turn the leaf ripe anew,
A promising fresh deal.
Breathe purely; live alive.
Your wide world left to feel.

Deserts scorched earth band.
Tropics dry, cracking around.
Poles of coolness walled.

Pass me a cold one,
So refreshing and sudsy.
Then we'll make a change.

The Easing of Wills

Hollowed by boundless changes,
Barren wastelands torched lie still.
Only found are some dry bones
With nothing left to kill.
Insisting deregulation,
Brash, gaslighted division
Flooding harmony with greed
Shouldn't be their decision.
To just accept the way it is,
Think you're unaccountable.
An example of passive guilt
Can be just as despicable.

False Hope

From the man up high,
Laws without compassion.
Kids treated like dogs
If from the wrong country.
Dividing our wills,
Perched from false worship,
Spewing hate and lies
Like how the One was.
They are enemies
To every person
With their destruction.
Redemption comes soon!

Believe

Some wield the light,
Paths formed just wide.
Others take shelter,
Defend their side.
See far what's now.
Parade so vast,
The dark—all else
Invades the past.
Believe within.
Empower your core.
Banish all lies,
And rise to endure!

Beware the regret.
Globally mixed blames confused.
Scorched plains, no return.

Russian Tang tastes bad.
We'll learn from this debacle,
None then to impede.

Hurry and Stop

So far from goodness we've been.
A great many went all in
To anoint a wildcard contrast.
They rejoice, blind to his sin.
His followers blow hot winds,
Winds of change, but change regressed.
"Let's come together," they'll say,
All "us" but the oppressed.
Some think it's from the news,
Aligns with the lies told.
But desperate as they are,
Fear is common; some just fold.
Boils down to intentions,
Ambitions, desires, goals.
What do the two sides stand for?
One money, one peace, and souls.
The rest are cogs in this blight,
Soaking up and soaking dry.
Certain few rarely even look back
As their wealth has 'em feelin' high.
So wake up, fellow people,
Hear the desperate cries to you.
We have just one planet.
Save these still skies of blue!

Time Flies

Workin', dazin', dreamin'
To finish with the bell.
Eyes ain't gonna focus;
Too much crap to quell.
Most of the things'll keep.
Won't pay no mind.
Guess I'll put it off
Until the next day's grind.

Going On

Color me a shaky-sure wisp,
Surely not conquered or overcome
Alive like aged twenty crisp.
And spare me steady wrinkles some.
Escapes my grasp, that great moment.
All is gone, 'cept the echo stays,
Grown resistant to torment.
What was all brown, now mostly grays.
Find my braver inner candle,
Cast from cozy safety ashore.
Blasts, high winds, born to handle.
Then, at once, all's in accord.
Into the blaze I now stare
With attention gone unspoken.
I'm unashamed to say I care.
My broken heart's now brave unbroken.

People drive asleep.
Others in the back caution
Gonna hit a tree.

Reward tomorrow
For our hard work today.
Great satisfaction.

Not so Fake

You must pardon my civility
As I vacate exclusivity,
All for heavenly harmony's sake.
But viewed by masses as simply fake.
Instead they stay aloof, dauntlessly
Veiled by walls constructed countlessly
Unaware of distance created,
When, in fact, we all are related.
Cousins far distanced by solitude.
Self-centered, making a harsh attitude.
Let's loosen delusion of control,
And let go enough to free the soul.
Newly freed, we own ourselves.
No longer caking dust on the shelves,
Now to see all spirits elated.
The present's where we're all created.

Currents

We are all bits and pieces,
Knowing little of it all.
Following steadily
Then making the call.
Starting anywhere, we roll
Bright and smart and good.
Outside that flow, quite bad.
None too understood.
The waves crash broadly,
Engulfing contrary posts
Through the air and water,
Leaving hungry ghosts.
The wonder we are victims
With fallen left for dead,
Blinded by fear of loss
Or that they won't be fed.
But we created this image
Following those above us.
Prop up those lacking morals,
Hoping they will love us.
This cycle is forever
Unless denial we suspend.
Stop bringing God into it.
On ourselves we must depend.

Fate I Follow

Way, way up in the distance,
Beyond what's normally seen,
A place bright, hopeful, and calm,
One that's surely ever clean.
Though a chance to fail is real,
It's no more than true success.
If belief to fail avoided
And I stop trying to impress.
Stay aligned within myself.
A prayer may be needed.
This willful faith lights my way.
Efforts must be repeated.
Having stayed true to myself,
Possibly only for the brave,
A decent chance made better
Whether or not this path I pave.
To ever give up seems wrong,
The guaranteed way to fail.
A notion like fighting nature
And that old "the earth's flat" tale.
Through this great journey we choose,
One which we each must discover,
We do what we think must be done
And realized before it's all over!

A path rutted, splayed.
Banal belief downtrodden.
Lost truths ancients knew.

Washed dreams found buried.
Strangled whispers seem untrue.
Yet it's the secret.

Shot in the Gut

In the jamb she watches
My squirms firmly in pain's grasp.
They arrive in batches.
From her, barely a gasp.
Flee far from my worn soul.
You deny my torture woke
This diamond turned to coal.
Steady strength for now be broke.
Truth be to bear distress,
To keep the love around.
Keep quiet and impress;
Is logic not so sound?
Brave, new, truth-seeing eyes,
Support and build love that's down.
You'd prove especially wise
When thorns pierce hard your crown.

Unique

Don't fret, don't run.
Don't fight, don't hate.
Anyone not of yours
Known as "them," "they."
Too fast, too quick.
Too bold, too blind.
We do look diverse
But with genes aligned.
We're hurt, we're felled.
We're lost, we're fools.
Our paths, each other's,
And not just smooth.
See more, see all.
See wills, see views.
With us each just one,
Not just selfless crews.

Embrace

Far spaced from our modern age,
Aloof from most others' plights,
To protect only that which was
When we enacted certain rights.
That narrow view isn't just
Counts those like the Fathers' offspring,
Omitting many out of fear.
"Give them rights, we're left with nothing!"
But look beyond this stepping stone.
Your neighbor seems a danger.
But mostly alike where it counts.
Only in this life are you strangers.
The mission doesn't stop with grace.
We must raze these walls enormous,
Expose our souls with inner strength,
These combined lights will transform us.

Lookin' out at you
And the like apathetic.
How are you happy?

Happiness for all.
Make more room for the others.
Giving is filling.

Dear Bosses

Need to rent a person's time
Founded on your appetites
And wanting us to give all,
No lack for material sights.
I work my wage diligent,
Above and beyond at times,
Not to be noticed or seen,
Just so I feel good inside.
A standard was created
By a type quite available.
Ones with most time to give
Hurt those without that timetable.
If a true effort is given,
Quality also is a must.
You cannot fire people
For being sick; it's not just!
Used up and then thrown away,
Workers recycled plenty.
They wouldn't dare ever care
If we starved ever so gently.

No Other Choice

You find yourself at odds,
Room's been closing in,
Suffering has its day
No matter where you've been.
The currents seem to swing
Back and forth, unending.
Distant hope teases 'til
Souls are done spending.
Now fight if you're strong.
Unless you want to quit.
So grab life by your will
And proclaim, "That's it!"

Sprout

Go, stray mind of wonder,
Eclipse eternal darkness.
Fighting none, meaning well,
A seemingly aped likeness.
Fade those worries, so finite.
There grows one true power,
That which comes from within.
Any false shading will sour.
Live for beauty of self
For this gift grows in triers.
Dreamers who make it out,
Walkers become flyers.

Doing a great job.
Days flyin' by infinite.
Better enjoy life.

Dark nights come to light
When silent ones turn aloud.
Thankful for this day.

Start Over

We must let it go,
The pain we carry.
And regrets also.
People do vary.
Unique path doldrums.
Darkness comes fully.
Light reaches the bottom.
Easy to sully.
Contacts close and away,
Online, anonymous.
Harsh, nasty thoughts sway
'Til hate's unanimous.
Deepened views entrenched,
We ride the centrifuge.
Due compromise is benched.
This skewed hate-fed deluge.
Awareness stops this trip.
Self-respect does hold.
Our parts we can't skip.
Diversity do behold.

In Me

All that time in the dark,
Lost, looking foolishly,
Countless attempts for air.
I go on endlessly.
My struggles seem in vain.
Fighting for full breaths,
Gaining little each time,
Causing terrible stress.
Through the storm and out,
Strong but worn entirely.
The light I sought so long
Was always inside me.

Faulty Man

This high post needs honor,
More than sly and shrewd,
To lead without fear,
Fair rationing food.
It means something else.
It's quite the honor,
Not some badge to flaunt:
King of the Manor!
No, and some do know
The duty inherent
To all needs this era.
For many, apparent.
So why do we insist
On raising the faulted,
Breaking all until
The world's breaths are halted?

Open

The cold outside world I see
Reflected back inside me.
Gazing too far I shake.
Gone past sane 'til me break.
Seers not seen so often,
Most shoot straight to the coffin.
Fly amassed toward that fate.
Time's now, maybe too late.
Whilst an acute pain grips most,
Taut wills take many a host.
Closed shutters, lost love,
Blind of what's always above.
Open, unintended, free, apart,
Connected bliss; life is art.
Wield your flame, feeling light.
Strength infused, shine so bright!

II

What It's All for and About

What life is for and about is up to each of us to discover on our own. I wanted to share part of what touched me most when I felt both well and not so well. I found my attention went from Mother Nature to a few random thoughts to love and pain, bringing to my attention what makes life so full and rich, regardless of money. I would like to point out one thing I truly love: rain. To me, a steady rain resets all the senses and clears the mind of stress and clutter, bringing near instant happiness. I also find it is the most conducive weather for meditation, with the constant sound of drops landing everywhere helping me find the right vibration to fly.

If we were all to find our centers and recognize that whole points of view exist in every other living thing, not just us, we can maybe find more consideration for one another. When this happens, we move closer to our current evolutionary potential, which is not just to avoid perishing from climate change or war, but partly to unlock more of our potential psychologically and socially. We would be best served working together as a planet, without the individualized governments currently creating selfish energy. And we had better do it fast.

When it comes to pain and love, both experiences are a major part in what creates you and shapes your development. We all hate the pain, of course, and sometimes to avoid it, we end up hurting another person. Then, sometimes we just take it, so someone else doesn't have to feel it. The biggest key to love working and keeping the pain minimal is first knowing yourself and the other person. Unfortunately, pain is inevitable as life happens. Just enjoy the thing in its entirety while it is here to be enjoyed.

A. Ma Nature

The beauty we see around and how we see it have always been an inspiration to me, changing from the full colors of a perfect spring day to the grayness of an October rainfall. It reminds me of the planet's living self, one of changing vitality, still pushing and pounding, but one that is off balance. I celebrate the purity of nature by pointing out what I treasure most about precipitation and the changing and returning of the seasons.

I still fail as I know what is felt by my skin—the brisk and fresh air of winter when the snow is falling, or the cooking torture of summer when the humidity is like soup—is only how I see it. That we all see things in our own way is why humanity has been able to evolve the way it has, and we are at the point where we can change how we treat our beloved planet and take care of each other with minimal pain.

Synchronizing with our surroundings, however we choose, is vital in our search for happiness, putting us in touch with depths beyond our imaginations and a better understanding that we are all connected. Trust in yourself and be free.

Sunset through the Trees

I gaze patiently from afar
Through the guarded trees,
The vastness of light diminished
But only from my worn seat.
The sun knows not my view,
And earth chooses its vantage.
When my day has ended,
The sun's day goes on.
The colors change as expected,
Fast through my spectrum
Until violet shows it's finished.
Can't help but be amazed.
Now the darkness overcomes
To take shelter in light's wake
As life is extinguished.
The light will be born again.

Sound of Snow

Perfect parade of white
Fractals wander awhile.
The smell of cold rushes;
My aura of heat broken.
Piercing senses, grand silence,
Quietly here, growing fast.
Such dense and thickened space.
The past's echoes heard no more.
Still felt strong, each touch draws,
Erases my world bright,
Miming untold emptiness.
Instead, it's sated fullness.
Positively negative.
Many yells falling short.
The calming cold eases me
With loud sights quite subtle.

Winter's Draw

In the breeze, they fall.
Cold, peaceful, still.
My breath so loud.
The air they fill.
Each floats in grace,
Falling alike high.
Gems of frost sparkle,
Crystals from the sky.
Timed sound rhythm,
Ripplin' waves dance.
A frozen ground
Is their only chance.

Through the arid cold,
My pilot light stays alit,
Swallowed in the snow.

A darling day bright.
Sun-bleached breezy aromas
Swaying my doldrums.

Spring

Go blow away, oh, frozen wind.
Thaw the harsh frost, become sweet dew.
Dead of winter, hopes are thinned.

All cold lets up, not so blue.
Critters awake, days get longer.
Feeling brighter and hopeful too.

From this journey, soul gets stronger.
Braved the cold suffer, life now alive.
No satisfaction, just hunger.

Flowers will bloom, all deep with pride,
As bees come 'round to do their deed.
This flower that 'til all are tried.

Birds start to sing; from cold they're freed.
Squirrels climb about; does birth fawns.
Life continues to spread its seed.

The bear awakens with giant yawns.
Feel the sun as spring now dawns.

Daybreak

The sun again breaks through,
Rays bursting life awake.
Birds calling each other,
All for their songs' sake.
Hills, towns lit lightly.
Tender life bares itself.
People rise for duties
And leave the place they dwell.
Brisk air, crisp and new,
No gusts, only peace,
Brushing my skin so fresh.
My spirit now free.

Drying Up

Swaying breezes still chilly.
Greens nourishing around,
Drying maybe just unseen,
Waiting calmly to be found.
The cold strangely remains
Until the break, that last drop.
Once flush drawn plenty moist,
Now cracked and stiff, drying up.

To feel the air's kiss,
Spring's attempt at winter's cold.
But look, now it's warm.

Cellar of wine choice,
Rich of sun's flavor true deep.
Drink always, still drunk.

Hotter

Still and arid hot,
With dust amid dew.
Focus now narrows,
Dreaming of fresh cool.
Swimming in the soup.
Not here out of choice.
The sun, no mercy,
It's now dried my voice.
Earth now facing strong,
With nary a wince.
Our star always blasts;
Dawn did give us hints.
Quite slow from fatigue,
Not such a hard ache.
It's just this damn heat
Feels like a slow bake.

Season of Relief

Ending are peak months,
Ones where veggies grow.
Now though, sweet relief.
Plenty of fruit now low.
Trees and bushes shed
Down to their bones
For sun's cold retreat.
They'll all remain alone.
From bone-dry and parched,
Salty, sticky, old
To coolness abound,
When smells dare be bold.
Take a giant breath.
Shows of life around.
The winds sweep chaos
With peace to be found.

Wet Soak

Flushing filling buckets,
Pouring, gushing loudly.
Wicked drenching nonstop.
Back to sleeping soundly.
Blinding, streaking lightning.
Calming downpour easing.
Waking crashing thunder.
Rain ideally pleasing.
Blessed water flowing,
Dousing dusty flaking,
Soothing, cooling, brewing.
My soul's yearly waking.

Now the sun's below.
The owl's howl gives an echo,
Spooky yet comfy.

Sing the morning light.
Birds converse in many tongues
Within the cool breeze.

Her Moods

Maybe admire all four,
Although I'm no guesser.
Our seasons are stacked
Like MC Escher.
Winter draws us in,
Making a sweet slumber.
Falling snow's serenity.
Cold draws you under.
Spring awakens hope,
Drawing sweet, lovely smells.
Animals come alive
And out of their shells.
Summer peaks desert heat,
Parching, tiring, tried treks.
Who'll be finding cover
Or feel reddened necks.
Fall comes, slowing, cooling.
Temperate-shrouded peace.
Steady rains ape spring.
Treasure times like these.
The cycle continues.
Cold, life, hot, and death loom,
Bringing us back and forth
Through nature's fickle moods.

A Walk

One step outside, two more.
I expect a stiff chill,
Not warmth this early.
Glad I have time to kill.
Back upstairs for a coat.
Grabbed a zip-up hoodie.
Then back to the sunshine.
This day seems a goody.
Down the street, strolling along,
I breathe the clean, fresh air.
Dip my head under a branch
Then held high without a care.
In the deli, got lotto.
Say hi to my foreign friends.
Brightest part of my day.
Hope our road never ends.
Back to walking, I go home.
For us, it's a lovely day.
But it's winter, far from sun,
Not supposed to be this way.

Planet Home

Blue, green, and brown hues,
Red tulips around.
Orange, yellow, purple,
Flowers sit proud.
Trees tall as could be.
Critters big and small,
Free and light as they may.
Beauty marks them all.
We owe all we are;
By respect we repay—
Instead of thick smog—
If we want to remain.
Air swiftly changing,
Processing the trees.
Our ways we'll alter,
And it won't be a breeze.
We reap what we sow.
Irony aloud too.
Life will cease to be
As earth starts anew.

A change comes to grow.
From dying, dry, and crusty,
Now fresh and vibrant.

Drops a globe of dew,
Like many true before it,
Refracting quaint scenes.

B. Somewhat Random Thoughts

Sometimes there are things that don't fit so neatly into a box, or close enough to force the top closed and forget about it; but there is a place for them. Random and abstract thoughts are paramount in creating a private haven for love and are dependent on each person's individuality, the very thing we need to avoid becoming drones of corporate profit or blinded by time's passing.

I am lucky to have multiple people—friends and family—I connect with and sometimes count on to keep me positive when life is a bit rough. Life can make you feel quite alone, but it's a tad bit easier just to know you're not alone.

So hold truth dear, but we must bend thought and discover our own zaniness, evolving beyond commonality to a living and dynamic world culture. Let go and be creative wherever you find yourself drawn. There is plenty of room for us all to bloom.

Half a Glass

If you had a drink
And want it filled,
Go all the way
Or bull be tilled.
But stop halfway,
Much confusion.
A clear path denies
This lil illusion.
Whilst the pour flows
This thought we mull.
Once we stop and look,
It's now half full.
Finish the pour.
Now please, in haste.
The glass you'll drink
With none to waste.
But stop halfway
Just to be witty.
It's obvious, right?
Your glass, half empty!

Cliché

A bird in the mouth is worth two in the hand.
It's not for the faint of mind.
You may have to take a knee to take a stand.
I will definitely keep an ear open.
Go the distance on half the gas.
See with all your senses.
Find peace and calm amidst chaos.
Take enough time to enjoy it.
Go all in, even if you don't take out.
Love deeply from the whole of your soul.
Keep close to mind those who suffer.
A sweet heart is a terrible thing to waste.

My Place

About this place I dwell …
Fairly center street.
Common to many for sure.
Still, to some elite.
Only two ways in here
Except the windows.
One door won't open;
The other won't close.
I prefer the front,
The one that welcomes.
It only gives you trouble;
Closing causes tantrums.
By virtue of my spot,
Side door, I might go.
Need to force it open.
Weirdly easy to close.
Either way's fine with me.
It might be subtle.
No matter the choice,
With both doors you struggle.

This highway drivin',
Ridin' lone, music blastin'.
Damn, ran outta gas.

Whimper weak wake up.
Stand strong; savor braver you.
Let loose lingered limp.

A dream unfolds, bloomed.
A lifetime of mystery.
A fate comes to pass.

Ab5tr4ct

Aplomb purple do pop.
Back down, end up, stop.
Hoops squad driven jazzy,
Trippin', flyin' snazzy.
Ramblin' red hummingbird.
Cars' squealin' wheels heard.
Clever find, a cat's boon,
Topped wonder to swoon.

Chocolate

It comes in pies or cakes,
Puddings and cordials,
Shop's ice cream specials.
Even tall milkshakes.
Some prefer candy,
Either milk or dark.
Nougat and bars,
They're rather dandy.
Liqueur, syrup, cookies.
When the chips are loose,
Rich and creamy mousse.
Sometimes solid bunnies.
But the things I like best
That have chocolate
Are those without it.
That's my only request!

Breakthrough

Kinder Rex and Cindy Plex,
Drinkin' mocha java joes.
Find his rug and then her jug.
Fight through mornin' woes.
Send him packin', jaw's slackin',
Awake and wired tired.
See the light, go make his plight,
If not to be admired.
Been up for days, counting ways
These tinker-timers be.
'Tis now dark, but not so stark,
The truth they come to see.
That it brings, that it sings,
Alive to live in love.
Soak it in when it begins
With nothing else to think of.

Scamper

Our souls scamper through time,
Living countless lives
With echoes ranged sublime.
Lake ripples from pebbles.
Some paths set before us,
Whether in stride or not,
Else ourselves we trust
Since an end we will meet.
We strive for stars aligned
Within our narrow views.
But all is found in kind
By finding your own rhythm.
Continue on your way
Along the thoroughfare,
And suffer love's great stay—
Purpose of the scamper.

C. To Suffer and Love

What I have found amid the worst era of my life, one of consistent disappointment and suffering, is a strength within strength. A force to pull through and try to give hope to others who suffer and want to give up, like I wanted to many times. We must push our own envelopes, and never fear growth.

The soul seems to have a limit. We feel like we break and cannot bear any more adversity. But we are pushed, and it seems we have no choice but to endure the worst. Those who quit and run will regret it. Those who stay and withstand the worst will flourish and do well to encourage growth in others. Not everyone is adequately equipped to handle their adversity, so we must find a way to account for everyone, or we will continue to suffer and lack balance.

Now, break out, and let go of the pain and worry that keep you in your rut. Focus on the things you love, and be ready and open for any possible outcome. Be open to the possibility of love, that sweet, lucid cloud of bliss that's quite hard to resist.

Pain

Calmness ruptures open raw,
Bearing life's brutal inner war.
Keen reminder we exist.
Hope resists it from afar.
Wreck my fragile frame unhinged.
Tear these tissues, clean rip.
Guard my diseased organs curled,
Forcing my patient last grip.
Wrack my aging middle mind.
Function less, so slippery.
Losing traction, trying my will.
Then gone, seen so gingerly.
Wring my spirit dispersed.
Tortured body, mind forgotten,
Both side by ugly side
Until all cells are rotten.
Wrestled free, presence gone,
Horrors breaking, chains crumble,
Body withers, returns.
Eternity, I am humble.

At Each End

I

Wow, to feel so at peace.
Will savor the moment.
You've been through this before.
Illusions will torment.
A misstep too early
And plummet beyond view,
Until rocky bottom
Of an ocean's deep blue.
Drowning my flooded mind,
No escape until relief
From this reality.
Gotta see through this fake grief.

II

A break that launches hard.
Tender soul skyward gone,
Again, beyond their view.
Thoughts light speed toggled on.
My labyrinth, so vast.
Unable to catch a breath,
This onslaught is quite cruel.
It's all been felt to death.
Agony wears you thin.
No relief, no comfort.
Must go lie down posthaste.
Peace be a slumber.

III

Within this struggle, a fall
Back down the deepest pit.
The soul now a yo-yo.
A life's work this won't fit.
Once past this obstacle,
Meditate what's outside
With directed breathing,
Centering what's inside.
Amid each inhale's gift
Some comfort, all fight.
Find your spirit endures
Far past any mind's plight.

Left

Years of love and anger,
Rolling glitter and gloom,
This joy's first breath kept strong.
Couldn't see impending doom.
My pains and hers askew,
Depths confused seemed akin.
Made me sway and lose sight.
And her, no way to forgive.
Parted, back on strange paths,
Our hopes disappear, free.
Remnants I was loved now gone
Until all that's left is me.

Breakdown

Agony scorching my soul.
Threats of a gutted depth,
My hopes disappear.
Gone.
Grief's barren fields yearn.
My faith and will to forfeit.
Still hold up strong.
Grind.
Karma built too twisted
As victim and culprit.
Lay me to waste.
Gray.
At onslaught's finale,
Erase me bitter, try.
Just me remains.
Grow.

Entombed

Simmering, bright fire,
Entombed spirit huff,
Torching torture torn.
Silence, deafness phased.
Pouring lava fills.
Grasping distant hope
Concentrates soul's might,
Drawing destined love.
Neutron purity, come.
Blessed, lovely cool.
Unending chaos calmed,
Lifting, bringing peace.

What am I to do?
Life coming at me full force.
I mustn't give in.

Welded mind forgets
Damaged breach in cohesion
Although more aware.

Hear the birdies chirp.
Difficult to pick apart.
Feel the harmony.

Overt, Caring Love

Souls come about that do prove daring
To race and chase until they banish hurt.
For all the wills saved, all done through sharing,
Saving a life from despair in the dirt.
Great burdens taken, seen as worth bearing.
You might imagine they'd give up their shirt.
Some evidence of great light from above,
This most wonderful, overt, caring love.

Born

Arriving just in time,
Barely able to breathe.
Can't see anything right.
Born now, I've come to be.
A moment pure to you,
But to me, forever
Catching every moment.
Bonding you can't sever.
A giant world awaits,
Blessed with life now no qualm.
Clueless wonder so pure.
Blind but see my perfect mom.

Give It a Try

If I'd be,
Then I'd see
The way free.
Try today.
Fly away.
Be okay.
Hold on tight.
Quite a sight
When just right.

Go

To be is to see.
To feel is to heal.
To know is to go.
To love is from above.

Love Is …

Love is belief indeed.
A divine, sprouting seed
Can grow tall, as assumed,
'Til all flowers have bloomed.
Light my soul, feed my life,
A gift shared above all strife.
The present ebbs and flows.
Rhythms the faithful arose.
Sure of aim to the core,
Its power we can score.
Must be open to pain
To drive down lovers' lane.
So open yourself true.
Feel the beauty you're due.
Without that little seed,
Love is a dream indeed.

Thinking love easy,
Dangerous notion learned late.
Laughing loud out loud.

Come, heavenly glow,
Part of nature's hold on me.
Bathe my soul in love.

Whisper sweet somethings,
Surfing tempting hot forces
Begs my surrender.

Awe

When I notice her,
There is no one other.
She draws me in more
Than I can utter.
Energy hits hard.
A blast of flavor,
Showing life withstood.
Surely hope to savor.
Depths of oceans held
God's great chaos tamed.
A spirit of beauty.
My heart is aflame!

No Way

No doubt in my mind
Could make it up.
But there's no way
She's not in love.
Her beauty pulls
This hopeless fool.
Ask for a date.
Nah, keep it cool.
The vibe, quite true.
Wouldn't dare push.
The store smells good.
Done if I rush.
Still overcome.
Full-on tingle.
She's quite exquisite.
No way she's single.
Back to back and forth.
Let her come to me?
I'll just take a chance.
That's the biggest key.

Tempted

Softest hi,
Tempting sigh.
Bring me light
Outta night.
Softest breath,
Draw my best,
Joining zen,
Always when.
Faint shiver,
Bliss giver,
Soft linen,
Hot friction.

Touch

Your soft touch glows,
Tingles my skin.
Quivers grow through,
Pushes from within.
Your aura glows,
Flushing my blood
Gently full red,
Beating my drum.
Your presence glows,
Melting my soul,
Quenching starkness.
Myself, the toll.

Swelter

Her beauty so sweet,
My heart takes a dive.
Whisper slow heat,
Lift my soul alive.
Your light touch warms,
Grazing smooth skin.
Our trembles in swarms.
Love your tempting grin.

Wonder of Life

Blessed bees,
Jumping roos,
Seeing trees,
Perching coos.
Wake at five,
Have a sip,
Feel alive,
Watch the hip.
Seen some scenes,
Furnished fits,
Stonewashed jeans,
Clever Brits.
Ride a wave.
Fly a kite.
Be so brave.
Love your life.

CPSIA information can be obtained
at www.ICGtesting.com
Printed in the USA
BVHW071226040119
537069BV00001B/32/P